RHINOS IN MY NOSE

The Chain of Infection

Written by
Morgan E. Giannelli

Illustrated by Jan Beeson
Edited by Jan Beeson

Copyright 2017
Illustration Copyright 2017
Library of Congress 2017

Published in the United States of America
ISBN 978-0-9890482-6-2

Proudly printed in the United States of America by
Lightning Source

Cover Design by Paul and Jan Beeson
Book design by Jan Beeson

Catalog - JNF024060 Juvenile nonfiction Health &
Daily Living - Personal Hygiene

This book is dedicated to my sons
Cashton & Parker
"Mommy loves you to the moon and back times infinity."

"I wish to thank my mom and step-dad, Paul, for their help with this book and my Mom, Paul, Dad and my Uncle Doug for their encouragement and support in my decision to become a great nurse. Love you all." Morgan

Hi there! My name is Nurse Morgan.

Today we are going to learn about..........
♫ DUN DUN DUNNNNNN! ♫

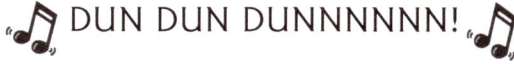

THE CHAIN OF INFECTION!

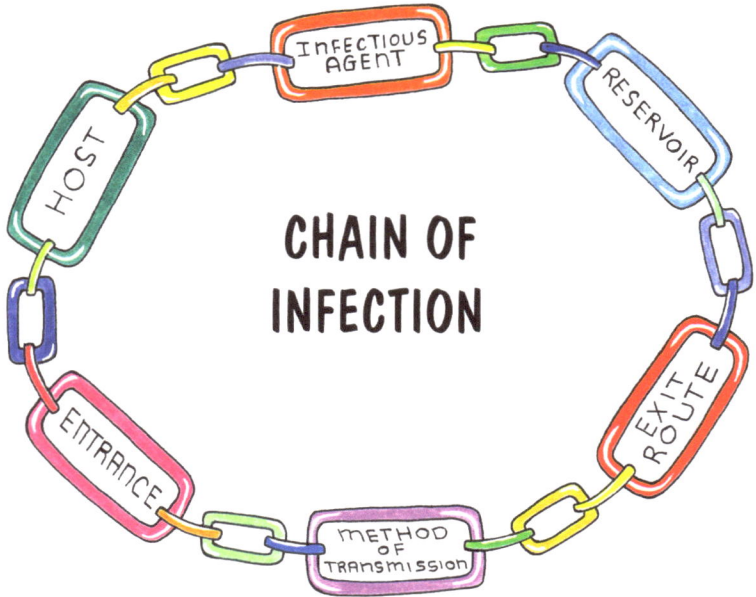

The chain of infection is made up of
six key elements.

So, put your learning caps on and let's go on an
educational trip that will help you to stay

HEALTHY.

The first key element in the chain of infection is the

INFECTIOUS AGENT

The Infectious Agent is a pathogenic microorganism such as bacteria, virus, yeast, fungi and protozoa. All of these microorganisms need fuel to grow and a suitable environment to survive. Let's take a look at a specific virus as it goes through .... "♫ DUN DUN DUNNNNNN! ♫

THE CHAIN OF INFECTION

THE INFECTIOUS AGENT
Rhinovirus aka the common cold

The second key element in the chain of infection is the
RESERVOIR
Infected human, animal or non-living source

In order to spread infection the microorganism must have a reservoir or "host." There are several different hosts; humans, animals and even non-living sources such as tables, door handles and medical equipment. Reservoirs need to create a hospitable atmosphere and food for the microorganisms to grow.

On a side note: humans and animals can carry viruses and not become ill but can still spread it. They are called "carriers" and "vectors." In this case however, animals cannot transmit the rhinovirus to humans because they carry their own type of viruses.

3

The third key element in the chain of infection is the

EXIT ROUTE

In order to infect someone else, the microorganism needs an exit route i.e., an escape from their current home.

In our case a runny nose, sneezing and coughing all cause secretions. Secretions are full of millions of tiny little rhinoviruses just waiting for their next victim.

The fourth key element in the chain of infection is the

METHOD OF TRANSMISSION
Vectors and Fomites

Once set out into the world these little buggers are
floating in the air, on your hands, tissues and surfaces.
If the surface is a living being it is called a "vector."
If it is an inanimate object it is called a "fomite."
A good rule of thumb is to practice good hand hygiene!!!
You can't spread the germs if you don't give them a
hospitable host.

Pick the "Vectors" and "Fomites."

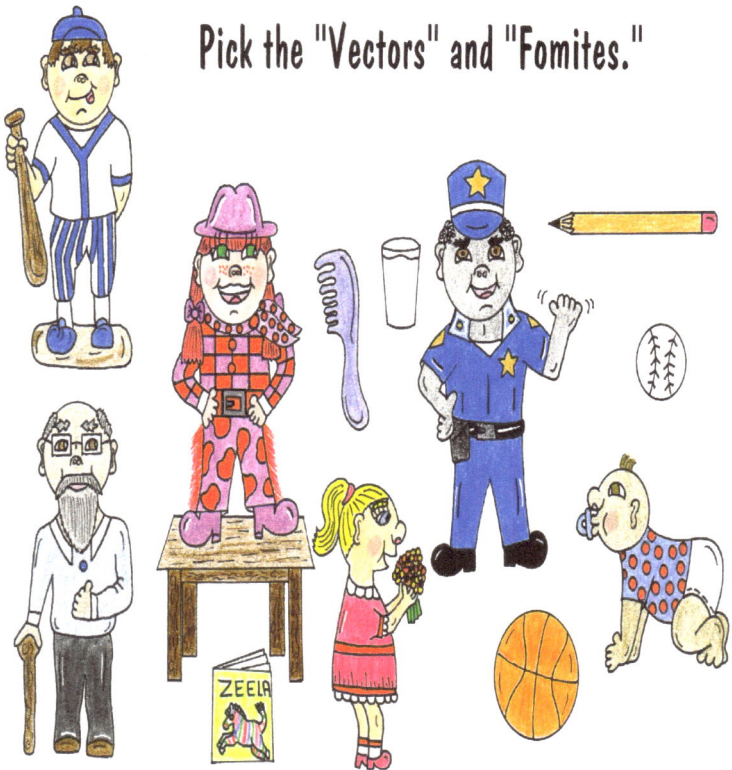

CAN YOU NAME OTHER "FOMITES?"

The fifth key element in the chain of infection is the

PORTAL OF ENTRY
Mouth, nose, cut in skin

Once it has found a suitable host all it needs is a tiny breakdown in the your skin, your mouth or the mucus membranes in your nose. Remember when I told you about practicing good hand hygiene? Well here is why!

Once the virus is out in the air or on a surface, you Mr. Dirty Hands picks up a tissue full of snot from an infected person and then neglects to wash his hands before dinner and BOOM, Mr. Rhinovirus has found itself a new host and is making himself comfy and cozy and rapidly reproducing in it's next victim. SO remember to always wash and dry your hands thoroughly.

The sixth key element in the chain of infection is the
HOST
Another person

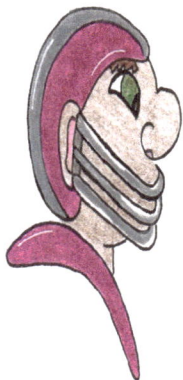

Let's take a small detour and talk about the stages of infection. The **Incubation Period** is the time between when the pathogen enters the body and the first symptoms start to appear.

With the common cold this could be 1 to 3 weeks. The host doesn't even realize they are sick and can infect others.

Next we have the **Prodromal Stage.** This is when non-specific signs and symptoms become more specific. The microorganism is rapidly multiplying and the host is more capable of spreading it to others and THEN things start to take a turn for the worse.

The **Acute Stage** is when the host develops all the signs and symptoms of the sickness. With the common cold our host will have a sore throat, sinus congestion, rhinitis and a high fever just to name a few. This is often the most contagious period.

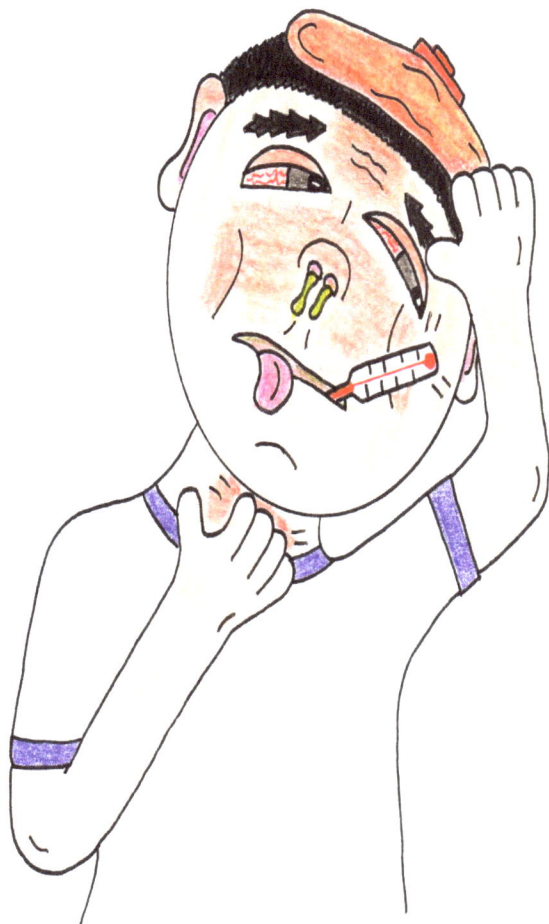

Just when you come to grips with your death, here comes the **Convalescence Stage.** The acute symptoms disappear and depending on your state of health you will start to recover in a few days.

Sadly, all of this could have been prevented with proper hand hygiene, covering your mouth when you sneeze with your arm instead of your hand, aka the "vampire cough" and properly disposing of soiled tissues can prevent the spread of infection.

This is called infection control and all you need to do is "break" one of the **Chains of Infection** we talked about above to prevent further transmission.

Now I know you're not a nurse but we can all practice asepsis. What is **ASEPSIS** you ask?

Asepsis is the absence of pathogenic microorganisms. There are two kinds of asepsis.

First we have **medical asepsis** or **"clean techniques."** This consists of basic techniques such as frequent, correct hand washing and in a nursing setting not shaking out dirty linens or placing them on the floor.

The other technique is **surgical asepsis** and is known as **"sterile technique"** and involves much more preparation and skill. It is used in specialized areas such as an operating room but also during invasive procedures such as catheterization. This technique kills all microorganisms and spores.

So! What did we learn here today? It is important to wash your hands and break the.....
♪ DUN DUN DUNNNNN! ♪
Chain of Infection.
One day it might not be just the common cold so practicing good hand hygiene is essential.

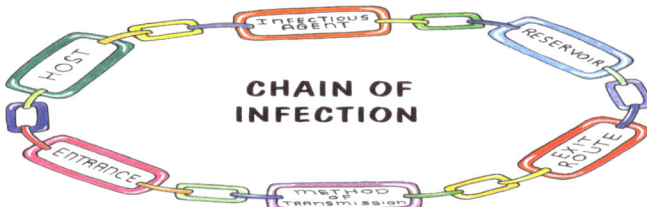

CHAIN OF INFECTION

GLOSSARY

A

acute - severe, critical, bad, serious

aka - also known as

B

bacteria - microscopic living organisms

C

catheterization - a thin tube made from medical grade materials used
for a broad range of functions

common - usual, ordinary, regular

E

elements - a component, part, section

environment - surroundings or conditions in which something lives

essential - absolutely necessary, extremely important

event - a thing that happens

F

fungi - a group of single-celled or multi-celled organisms that live by
decomposing and absorbing the organic material where they grow

H

hospitable - pleasant and favorable

hygiene - doing things to help prevent disease through cleanliness

I

inanimate - not alive

infection - the process of a virus or disease

invasive - involving the use of instruments or other objects into the body

O

organic - living matter

organism - an individual animal, plant or single-celled life form

P

pathogen - a bacterium, virus or other microorganism that can cause
        disease

R

reservoir - a place where fluid collects

rhinitis - inflammation of the mucus membrane of the nose caused by
        a virus infection

S

specific - clearly defined, particular

suitable - acceptable or satisfactory

survive - continue to live or exist

symptoms - signs of illness; fever, cough, etc.

T

technique - skill, ability

thrive - prosper, flourish, do well

transmit - cause something to pass on from one person or place to
        another

V

virus - an infective agent that multiplies only in a living host

Y

yeast - single-celled microorganisms in the fungi family

www.ingramcontent.com/pod-product-compliance
Lightning Source LLC
Chambersburg PA
CBHW040805040426
42339CB00013B/1